This book is a

Gift

From

....

To

....

Date

....

May God bless you through this book

DELIVERANCE FROM LUKEWARMNESS

PRAYER M. MADUEKE

Prayer Publications

PRAYER PUBLICATIONS

15, Olumo Street, Onike, Yaba, Lagos State, Nigeria.
46, Adelabu Street, Uwani, Enugu State, Nigeria.
+234 803 353 0599

DELIVERANCE FROM LUKEWARMNESS

Copyright © 2018

PRAYER M. MADUEKE

ISBN:

Prayer Publications

Unless otherwise indicated, all Scripture quotations are taken from the King James Version of the Bible, and used by permission. All emphasis within quotations is the author's additions.

First Edition, 2018

For further information of permission

46, Adelabu Street, Uwani, Enugu State, Nigeria.

15, Olumo Street, Onike, Yaba, Lagos State, Nigeria.

+234 803 353 0599

Email: prayermadu@yahoo.com,

Website: www.prayermadueke.com

AN INVITATION TO BECOME A MINISTRY PARTNER

In response to several calls from readers of my books on how to partner with this ministry, we are grateful to provide our ministry's bank details.

Be assured that our continued prayers for you will be answered according to God's word. And as you remain faithful by sowing seeds of faith, God will never forget your labours of love in Christ.

IN NIGERIA & AFRICA

Send your seed to:

Bank: Access Bank

Account Name: Prayer Emancipation Missions

Account Number: 0692638220

IN THE UNITED STATES AND THE REST OF THE WORLD

Bank: Wells Fargo - Bank

Account Name: Madueke P Madueke

Account Number: 7661203070

Routing Number (RTN): 055003201

Table of Contents

INTRODUCTION

D eliverance as a definite topic is not easily exhaustible. Most Christians do not consider the issue of personal deliverance as a duty they owe themselves. With an excellent understanding of personal deliverance, a Christian can be sure to live a victorious Christian life; not that which is void of battles of life but that with victories over life's great battles.

WHAT IS PERSONAL DELIVERANCE?

- Personal deliverance involves destroying the effects of bloodline curses (see Genesis 34:25-31; 49:3-7; 2 Samuel 21:1-9).

- It is seeking to have victory over defeat one's parents suffered (see Joshua 7:1; 8:1-29).

- It is to gather your blessings or to recover scattered and stolen blessings from enemies.

Deliverance is recovering your loss, things your ancestors handed over to evil powers through sin, evil sacrifices, curses or evil covenants (see Jeremiah 16:1-4, 10-12). On the other hand, it is also important to state that deliverance is further divided into two major parts namely:

- Deliverance from sin (see John 3:16, 32, 36).

- Deliverance from the consequences of sin, physical infirmities or problems (see Matthew 10:28).

DISCOVERY OF ONESELF

Simply put, personal deliverance is a direct discovery of oneself and problems one is battling through life. This can be revealed as God guides you in times of Bible study, through vision, dream or through prayers.

God can help you discover your true self through His Word. For this purpose, go beyond reading this book ordinarily to pursuing an in-depth study of all scriptural references to see if you could discover your problems together with right prayers to pray. This book offers right prayers you can pray to achieve desired results.

Here are important things you must do:

- You must discover besetting sinful habits, repent from them and turn wholly to God through Jesus Christ, the Savior (see Matthew 11:28-30; John 1:40-42, 45-47, Acts 8:26-37).

- You must prepare for a personal experience and relationship with Jesus Christ as your Savior and Lord.

I can write some prayers for you as a guide but if you could discover the right prayers yourself, it would be better than what anyone else could write down for you.

Doctors have discovered that getting patients participate in their healing process through a technique called occupational therapy have had tremendous and remarkable effects on such patients. Likewise, you must be prepared to affect your deliverance through thoughtful and deliberate actions that could help trigger your deliverance.

Before you go into the study of this book, even if you have been born-again for long, make your assurance double sure and pray this prayer:

Almighty God, I know I have broken Your laws and my sins have separated me from You. I am truly sorry, and now I turn away from my past sinful habits and evils towards You. Please forgive me and help me to avoid sinning again. I invite Jesus Christ into my life to become the Lord of my life, to rule and reign in my heart forever from this day forward. Please send Your Holy Spirit to help me obey You, and to do Your will for the rest of my life, in the name of Jesus, Amen.

Having prayed the above prayer, pick your writing material and write down what you hope to discover about your life through the study of this book and the areas you need prayers of deliverance as you study this book. Make a list of all your problems and your needs. There are two ways to pray: 1. *You talk to God directly*, and 2. *You talk to your problem or the powers behind them.*

This book is divided into 34-part series to enable you study them easily. People read just to get information but when you want to get real knowledge or have understanding, experience and instruction, you need to study or learn. You need to give these 34-part series a required attention. You have to make out enough time, engage in this study and consider attentively each title in details to plot out, design and write down all you need to do in other to obtain your deliverance.

If you still want me to be in agreement with you through prayers, you can call me or just mention my name in agreement, as you pray after the program. God bless you and give you understanding as you go into this study, in the mighty name of Jesus.

CHAPTER - 1

THE ETERNAL LIVING CHRIST

This is the last of the seven churches in Asia addressed by Christ, the head and shepherd of the church. These churches actually existed at that time and they had typical and prophetic significance. The churches typify different types of churches today and they prophetically represent churches at all times, in all lands and of all church ages. The Laodicea church had no point of praise or commendation. It was, no doubt the last and the worst of all the churches.

Religion becomes a substitute for reality and Luke warmness characterized the whole church. There was not even the trace of a faithful few as in Sradis. Yet, the Lord is pictured as standing at the door of every heart, knocking and asking for entrance. What a wonderful love from the Lord who died for all, willing to save, ready to cleanse.

Christ the author, the origin of the book of Revelation is also the great counselor to all the churches. In the letter to the seven churches, He manifested the whole characteristics in its entirety. Our living eternal Christ, the great and living Savior, the first and the last, who is before the changing circumstances of life, with the final authority writes again to the seventh church in Asia.

> 'And unto the angel of the church of the Laodiceans write; These things saith the Amen, the faithful and true witness, the beginning of the creation of God' (Revelation 3:14).

> 'Jesus saith unto him, I am the way, the truth, and the life: no man cometh unto the Father, but by me' (John 14:6).

Each letter began with great attributes, characteristics and titles of Jesus Christ. "Amen" means verily, certainly or so be it, a guarantee or affirmation of the truth of a statement. He is the faithful and true witness and His words are final without question. He is the beginning and the end, the guarantor of every promise of God. Christ as the faithful witness seals every promise that God made in the scriptures. He is the beginning of the creation of God, which means, the origin, the author, the first cause of creation. He is the way, the truth and the life, the last person before God the father.

> 'In the beginning was the Word, and the Word was with God, and the Word was God. The same

was in the beginning with God. All things were made by him; and without him was not anything made that was made. In him was life; and the life was the light of men' (John 1:1-4).

In the beginning, the word appeared and the word was with God, and the word was God. Christ is the word, is always with God, and cannot be separated from the word because He was the word and the word was God. No one can have God without the word and to reject Christ is to reject God, who is the word.

'And to know the love of Christ, which passeth knowledge, that ye might be filled with all the fullness of God' (Ephesians 3:9).

'For by him were all things created, that are in heaven, and that are in earth, visible and invisible, whether they be thrones, or dominions, or principalities, or powers: all things were created by him, and for him: And he is before all things, and by him all things consist. And he is the head of the body, the church: who is the beginning, the firstborn from the dead; that in all

things he might have the preeminence'
(Colossians 1:16-18).

God appeared through Christ when He created the world through Him and came to the world through Him to have fellowship with us. It was by Him that all things were created, both things in heaven, things on earth, visible and invisible. Every throne, dominion, principalities and powers, all came through Him and are under Him and for Him. Therefore, He is before all things and by Him, all things consist and come to be. He is the leader, in charge and the head of every head and nothing that had begun was begun without Him, His approval or knowledge. Christ was the first-born, the beginning and the prominence of all things. No one can ignore Him and succeed and no success is a success without Him.

'But as God is true, our word toward you was not yea and nay. For the Son of God, Jesus Christ, who was preached among you by us, even by me and Silvanus and Timotheus, was not yea and nay, but in him was yea. For all the promises

of God in him are yea, and in him Amen, unto the glory of God by us (2 Corinthians 1:18-20).

Truth starts with Christ and any church or individual that has no Christ, has no truth and any preaching that does not embrace the truth of Christ is not complete. Without Him, there will be no fulfillment of any promise because He is the Amen or so be it, a seal to every Amen.

'And unto the angel of the church of the Laodiceans write; These things saith the Amen, the faithful and true witness, the beginning of the creation of God (Revelation 3:14).

'For I would that ye knew what great conflict I have for you, and for them at Laodicea, and for as many as have not seen my face in the flesh' (Colossians 2:1).

LET US TALK ABOUT THE CITY OF LAODIEA:

Laodicea was a rich city and the chief city in Phrygia, founded about 250 B.C. by Antiochus the second and named after his wife. It was 45 miles S.E. of Philadelphia and about 40 miles from Ephesus. It was not far from

Colossi and Hierapolis. It had a very large Jewish population and also had a medical center. The Apostle Paul knew this church of Laodicea and had a great concern and love for the church. Epaphras, a servant of Christ had a great zeal for the brethren, which were in Laodicea, desiring and praying that they would be perfect and complete in all the will of God.

> 'For I would that ye knew what great conflict I have for you, and for them at Laodicea, and for as many as have not seen my face in the flesh; That their hearts might be comforted, being knit together in love, and unto all riches of the full assurance of understanding, to the acknowledgement of the mystery of God, and of the Father, and of Christ' (Colossians 2:1-2).

Paul, an apostle of Jesus Christ had previously written to them. The condition of the church moved him to pray for them, desiring that they work together in unity, divine love and to be exposed to the mystery of Christ. Epaphras fervently prayed for them and called them by name in prayer.

'Epaphras, who is one of you, a servant of Christ, saluteth you, always labouring fervently for you in prayers that ye may stand perfect and complete in all the will of God. For I bear him record, that he hath a great zeal for you, and them that are in Laodicea, and them in Hierapolis. Salute the brethren, which are in Laodicea, and Nymphas, and the church which is in his house... And when this epistle is read among you, cause that it be read also in the church of the Laodiceans; and that ye likewise read the epistle from Laodicea' (<u>Colossians 4:12-13, 16</u>).

The church in Laodicea was so privileged to receive and read many copies of letters from other great men of God before the present one that we are reading now. But by the time Christ address them in Revelation chapter three through the Apostle John, about 35 years later, the church had completely become lukewarm and backslidden.

CHAPTER - 2

THE LUKEWARM CONGREGATION

What does it mean to be lukewarm, neither cold nor hot? Does it mean to be spiritually weak, feeble, tempted or of little strength? No. A bruised reed shall he not break and smoking flax shall he not quench.

> 'A bruised reed shall he not break, and smoking flax shall he not quench, till he send forth judgment unto victory' (Matthew 12:20).

> 'For we have not an high priest which cannot be touched with the feeling of our infirmities; but was in all points tempted like as we are, yet without sin' (Hebrews 4:15).

If these were only weak, feeble and discouraged, Christ with divine gentleness and sympathy would have encouraged and strengthen them rather than rebuking and chastising them. They were wretched, miserable, poor, blind and naked spiritually. It was a congregation of sinners and backsliders professing to be Christians. They were vile and sinful, pitiable and without the robe of righteousness. They were insincere, religious hypocrites and harder to win to Christ than cold, irreligious sinners.

'(But this spake he of the Spirit, which they that believe on him should receive: for the Holy Ghost was not yet given; because that Jesus was not yet glorified.) Many of the people therefore, when they heard this saying, said, Of a truth this is the Prophet. Others said, This is the Christ. But some said, Shall Christ come out of Galilee?' (John 7:39-41).

There are some members of the church which are nonchalant and can never be moved, no matter the move of God in their midst. They come to church but will not contribute positively or show concern. They are just on the fence, doing nothing.

'And when he was come into the temple, the chief priests and the elders of the people came unto him as he was teaching, and said, By what authority doest thou these things? And who gave thee this authority? And Jesus answered and said unto them, I also will ask you one thing, which if ye tell me, I in likewise will tell you by what authority I do these things. The baptism of John, whence was it? From heaven, or of men?

And they reasoned with themselves, saying, If we shall say, From heaven; he will say unto us, Why did ye not then believe him? But if we shall say, Of men; we fear the people; for all hold John as a prophet. And they answered Jesus, and said, We cannot tell. And he said unto them, Neither tell I you by what authority I do these things. But what think ye? A certain man had two sons; and he came to the first, and said, Son, go work today in my vineyard. He answered and said, I will not: but afterward he repented, and went. And he came to the second, and said likewise. And he answered and said, I go, sir: and went not. Whether of them twain did the will of his Father? They say unto him, The first. Jesus saith unto them, Verily I say unto you, That the publicans and the harlots go into the kingdom of God before you. For John came unto you in the way of righteousness, and ye believed him not: but the publicans and the harlots believed him: and ye, when ye had seen it, repented not afterward, that ye might believe him' (Matthew 21:23-32).

Religious people are very knowledgeable and they know many things but they do not have relationship with God through Christ. They are faultfinders, always looking for an excuse to accuse the righteous. When I was growing up in my village, I discovered two groups of people, idol worshippers and church people. Christians and none Christians, unbelievers and believers. It was clearly defined to the understanding of even a fool. The church people, believers or Christians were collection of those who are called of God to be His children and they responded, purchased, cleansed from sin and their names written in heaven.

> 'Take heed therefore unto yourselves, and to all the flock, over the which the Holy Ghost hath made you overseers, to feed the church of God, which he hath purchased with his own blood' (Acts 20:28).

These sets of believers in my village are visible church Christians. They are the assembly of people who are saved and they usually come together regularly to worship and fellowship

'A new commandment I give unto you, That ye love one another; as I have loved you, that ye also love one another. By this shall all men know that ye are my disciples, if ye have love one to another' (John 13:34-35).

'Moreover if thy brother shall trespass against thee, go and tell him his fault between thee and him alone: if he shall hear thee, thou hast gained thy brother. But if he will not hear thee, then take with thee one or two more, that in the mouth of two or three witnesses every word may be established. And if he shall neglect to hear them, tell it unto the church: but if he neglect to hear the church, let him be unto thee as an heathen man and a publican' (Matthew 18:15-17).

They are saved from their sins, separated from the world; they were always in fellowship with God, and with one another. Many of them were poor but they were always happy, without worry and anxiety. They have definite relationship with Christ. They go to church and regular bible studies, fellowships, prayers and soul winning were their hallmark. In their meeting days, bible studies, they assemble to study, learn, love, learn how to lean on God. The lives of all their members glorify God, keep bible doctrines and preach to none members. They worship God together, care for others, especially their members. They were faithful at home, at work and prayerful at all time

'And they continued stedfastly in the apostles' doctrine and fellowship, and in breaking of bread, and in prayers' (Acts 2:42).

'Obey them that have the rule over you, and submit yourselves: for they watch for your souls, as they that must give account, that they may do it with joy, and not with grief: for that is unprofitable for you' (Hebrews 13:17).

'And he gave some, apostles; and some, prophets; and some, evangelists; and some, pastors and teachers. For the perfecting of the saints, for the work of the ministry, for the edifying of the body of Christ' (Ephesians 4:11-12).

'Therefore they that were scattered abroad went everywhere preaching the word' (Acts 8:4).

'Let as many servants as are under the yoke count their own masters worthy of all honor, that the name of God and his doctrine be not blasphemed. And they that have believing masters, let them not despise them, because they are brethren; but rather do them service, because they are faithful and beloved, partakers of the benefit. These things teach and exhort' (1Timothy 6:1).

'Exhort servants to be obedient unto their own masters, and to please them well in all things; not answering again; Not purloining, but shewing all good fidelity; that they may adorn the doctrine of God our Savior in all things' (Titus 2:9-10).

'I will therefore that men pray everywhere, lifting up holy hands, without wrath and doubting' (1Timothy 2:8).

'Pray without ceasing' (1Thessalonians 5:17).

THEY ARE LIKE A FAMILY

'Of whom the whole family in heaven and earth is named' (Ephesians 3:15).

LIKE A FLOCK

'Take heed therefore unto yourselves, and to all the flock, over the which the Holy Ghost hath made you overseers, to feed the church of God, which he hath purchased with his own blood' (Acts 20:28).

LIKE A VINEYARD

'For we are laborers together with God: ye are God's husbandry, ye are God's building' (1Corinthians 3:9).

AND A NATION

'But ye are a chosen generation, a royal priesthood, an holy nation, a peculiar people; that ye should shew forth the praises of him who hath called you out of darkness into his marvelous light' (1Peter 2:9).

Each member's life is determined by their spiritual experiences, love, faith, prayer life, knowledge and obedience. They do not joke with church attendance and their membership. Their members are saved from sin and they live new life

> 'But ye are not in the flesh, but in the Spirit, if so be that the Spirit of God dwell in you. Now if any man have not the Spirit of Christ, he is none of his' (Romans 8:9).

> 'Know ye not, that to whom ye yield yourselves servants to obey, his servants ye are to whom ye obey; whether of sin unto death, or of obedience unto righteousness? But God be thanked, that ye were the servants of sin, but ye have obeyed from the heart that form of doctrine, which was delivered you. Being then made free from sin, ye became the servants of righteousness. I speak after the manner of men because of the infirmity of your flesh: for as ye have yielded your members servants to uncleanness and to iniquity unto iniquity; even

so now yield your members servants to righteousness unto holiness' (<u>Romans 6:17-19</u>).

They also preach to people, none members everywhere. When they came together to fellowship, they sing and clap hands. They pray and most times, speak in tongues. Once you join their group and hear their preaching during bible study, obey and accept Christ, your parents, neighbors, school people, office, market place will know. Everywhere you go, people will quickly know that you have joined the group. Your dressing, way of life, behavior, everything about you will immediately change. Your friends, relationships with others will change.

People will call you born-again, Scripture Union (S.U), and they will begin to persecute you, call you names. Your parents, helpers will deny you of your rights, try to stop you. They called this group, Pentecostals, born again, hand clappers or people who get drunk with American drugs or charms.

The second group is churchgoers or idol worshipers. Some of them go to church and worship idol. Others go to church but they do not worship idol or physically

enter into shrines. They are not outright idol worshippers, they go to church but they do not have power over sin. They are not born again, though they are baptized and given Christian names. In their church, they do not clap hands, speak in tongue or carry bible like Pentecostals those days.

While Pentecostal members, believers or born again answer Christ's call through hearing God's words, repentance, confession and forsaking of their sins, the other group answer their own call by being baptized and belonging to their church. The Pentecostal of those days get born-again; forsake sin, Satan, self to follow Christ, the Savior. They turn away from darkness to walk in the light. They enter into narrow gate to walk in the narrow way. In their bible study times, they are instructed to walk worthy of their call of salvation. Their characters change as they become members of the body of Christ

'I therefore, the prisoner of the Lord, beseech you that ye walk worthy of the vocation wherewith ye are called' (Ephesians 4:1).

'*Then spake Jesus again unto them, saying, I am the light of the world: he that followeth me shall not walk in darkness, but shall have the light of life*' (<u>John 8:12</u>).

'*Therefore we are buried with him by baptism into death: that like as Christ was raised up from the dead by the glory of the Father, even so we also should walk in newness of life*' (<u>Romans 6:4</u>).

'*This I say therefore, and testify in the Lord, that ye henceforth walk not as other Gentiles walk, in the vanity of their mind, Having the understanding darkened, being alienated from the life of God through the ignorance that is in them, because of the blindness of their heart: Who being past feeling have given themselves over unto lasciviousness, to work all uncleanness with greediness. But ye have not so learned Christ*' (<u>Ephesians 4:17-20</u>).

'*Only let your conversation be as it becometh the gospel of Christ: that whether I come and see you, or else be absent, I may hear of your affairs, that ye stand fast in one spirit, with one mind striving together for the faith of the gospel'* (Philippians 1:27).

'Brethren, be followers together of me, and mark them which walk so as ye have us for an ensample. (For many walk, of whom I have told you often, and now tell you even weeping, that they are the enemies of the cross of Christ: Whose end is destruction, whose God is their belly, and whose glory is in their shame, who mind earthly things.)' (Philippians 3:17-19).

'That ye might walk worthy of the Lord unto all pleasing, being fruitful in every good work, and increasing in the knowledge of God' (Colossians 1:10).

They are taught that in relationship with others in the church, at home and in the society, their new life and new walk must show:

LOWLINESS

'With all lowliness and meekness, with longsuffering, forbearing one another in love' (Ephesians 4:2).

'Let nothing be done through strife or vainglory; but in lowliness of mind let each esteem other better than themselves. Look not every man on his own things, but every man also on the things of others. Let this mind be in you, which was also in Christ Jesus' (Philippians 2:3-5).

'Took branches of palm trees, and went forth to meet him, and cried, Hosanna: Blessed is the King of Israel that cometh in the name of the Lord. And Jesus, when he had found a young ass, sat thereon; as it is written, Fear not, daughter of Sion: behold, thy King cometh, sitting on an ass's colt. These things understood not his disciples at the first: but when Jesus was glorified, then remembered they that these things were written of him, and that they had done these things unto him. The people therefore that was with him when he called

Lazarus out of his grave, and raised him from the dead, bare record' (John 12:13-17).

'And to offer a sacrifice according to that which is said in the law of the Lord, A pair of turtledoves, or two young pigeons. And, behold, there was a man in Jerusalem, whose name was Simeon; and the same man was just and devout, waiting for the consolation of Israel: and the Holy Ghost was upon him. And it was revealed unto him by the Holy Ghost, that he should not see death, before he had seen the Lord's Christ' (Luke 22:24-26).

MEEKNESS

'With all lowliness and meekness, with longsuffering, forbearing one another in love' (Ephesians 4:2).

'Take my yoke upon you, and learn of me; for I am meek and lowly in heart: and ye shall find rest unto your souls' (Matthew 11:29).

'*Put on therefore, as the elect of God, holy and beloved, bowels of mercies, kindness, humbleness of mind, meekness, longsuffering; Forbearing one another, and forgiving one another, if any man have a quarrel against any: even as Christ forgave you, so also do ye*' (Colossians 3:12-13).

'*To speak evil of no man, to be no brawlers, but gentle, shewing all meekness unto all men*' (Titus 3:2).

LONGSUFFERING

'*With all lowliness and meekness, with longsuffering, forbearing one another in love*' (Ephesians 4:2).

'*Charity suffereth long, and is kind; charity envieth not; charity vaunteth not itself, is not puffed up, Doth not behave itself unseemly, seeketh not her own, is not easily provoked, thinketh no evil; Rejoiceth not in iniquity, but rejoiceth in the truth*' (1 Corinthians 13:4-6).

'Giving no offence in anything, that the ministry be not blamed: But in all things approving ourselves as the ministers of God, in much patience, in afflictions, in necessities, in distresses, In stripes, in imprisonments, in tumults, in labours, in watchings, in fastings; By pureness, by knowledge, by longsuffering, by kindness, by the Holy Ghost, by love unfeigned, By the word of truth, by the power of God, by the armor of righteousness on the right hand and on the left, By honor and dishonor, by evil report and good report: as deceivers, and yet true; As unknown, and yet well known; as dying, and, behold, we live; as chastened, and not killed; As sorrowful, yet always rejoicing; as poor, yet making many rich; as having nothing, and yet possessing all things' (2 Corinthians 6:3-10).

He can boldly discuss this with the Corinthians because of his devotion to them

'O ye Corinthians, our mouth is open unto you, our heart is enlarged. Ye are not straitened in us, but ye are straitened in your own bowels. Now

for a recompence in the same, (I speak as unto my children,) be ye also enlarged. Be ye not unequally yoked together with unbelievers: for what fellowship hath righteousness with unrighteousness? And what communion hath light with darkness? And what concord hath Christ with Belial? Or what part hath he that believeth with an infidel? And what agreement hath the temple of God with idols? For ye are the temple of the living God; as God hath said, I will dwell in them, and walk in them; and I will be their God, and they shall be my people' (2 Corinthians 6:11-16).

FORBEARANCE

'With all lowliness and meekness, with longsuffering, forbearing one another in love... And be ye kind one to another, tenderhearted, forgiving one another, even as God for Christ's sake hath forgiven you' (Ephesians 4:2, 32).

'Forbearing one another, and forgiving one another, if any man have a quarrel against any: even as Christ forgave you, so also do ye' (Colossians 3:13).

LOVE

'With all lowliness and meekness, with longsuffering, forbearing one another in love' (Ephesians 4:2).

'Be ye therefore followers of God, as dear children; And walk in love, as Christ also hath loved us, and hath given himself for us an offering and a sacrifice to God for a sweetsmelling savor' (Ephesians 5:1-2).

'We love him, because he first loved us. If a man say, I love God, and hateth his brother, he is a liar: for he that loveth not his brother whom he hath seen, how can he love God whom he hath not seen? And this commandment have we from him, That he who loveth God love his brother also' (1John 4:19-21).

UNITY WITH THE CHURCH

'Blessed be the God and Father of our Lord Jesus Christ, who hath blessed us with all spiritual blessings in heavenly places in Christ' (Ephesians 4:3).

'Neither pray I for these alone, but for them also which shall believe on me through their word; That they all may be one; as thou, Father, art in me, and I in thee, that they also may be one in us: that the world may believe that thou hast sent me. And the glory which thou gavest me I have given them; that they may be one, even as we are one: I in them, and thou in me, that they may be made perfect in one; and that the world may know that thou hast sent me, and hast loved them, as thou hast loved me' (John 17:20-23).

'For as the body is one, and hath many members, and all the members of that one body, being many, are one body: so also is Christ. For by one Spirit are we all baptized into one body, whether we be Jews or Gentiles, whether *we be bond or free; and have been all made to drink into one Spirit. For the body is not one member, but many. If the foot shall say, Because I am not the hand, I am not of the body; is it therefore not of the body? And if the ear shall say, Because I am not the eye, I am not of the body; is it therefore not of the body? If the whole body were an eye, where were the hearing? If the whole were hearing, where were the smelling? But now hath God set the members every one of them in the body, as it hath pleased him'* (1Corinthians 12:12-18).

'That there should be no schism in the body; but that the members should have the same care one for another' (1Corinthians 12:25).

PEACE AMONG EACH OTHER

'Endeavouring to keep the unity of the Spirit in the bond of peace' (Ephesians 4:3).

'Follow peace with all men, and holiness, without which no man shall see the Lord' (Hebrews 12:14)

'And the servant of the Lord must not strive; but be gentle unto all men, apt to teach, patient' (2 Timothy 2:24).

'Recompense to no man evil for evil. Provide things honest in the sight of all men. If it be possible, as much as lieth in you, live peaceably with all men' (Romans 12:17-18).

I remember those days, as a young born again, new convert, immediately we finished bible study for the day, with zeal, I will go into my bible, repeat the bible quotations, read it over and over and examine my life with those bible references. Anyone I do not understand, I will go to my pastor, any leader and ask question. I make note of every bible study.

In fact, what I am telling you now is from my old bible study notebook, taught by my first Pastor Kumuyi at Gbagada Deeper Life Bible Church Gbagada, 1984. As we leave the church from every fellowship, we come out to practice it before our parents, schoolmates, neighbors, fellow believers and anyone around us. We use the bible to test ourselves to see if we are really born again. We watch how we react when others provoke us, tell lies against us.

We are happy when we suffer or denied our rights because of Christ. Those days, membership was not a mixture of wheat and tares but only those who were purchased with His own blood (*see* Acts 20:28). Church attendance and church membership are two different things. True church members hate sins; ignore sins, treats sins in the midst of sinners as if they do not exist. But people who just attend church respond to sin, play with sin and are alive to sin. Truly born-again church members are dead to sin and do not respond to the demands of the flesh. A nation does not count the dead and foreigners when citizens are being counted. Neither does a family count the dead and the fetus as part of the family. It is proper, legitimate, necessary and helpful for any church to know their members provided the dead; the foreigners and the fetus are not counted

'Then they that gladly received his word were baptized: and the same day there were added

unto them about three thousand souls' (Acts 2:41).

'Howbeit many of them which heard the word believed; and the number of the men was about five thousand' (Acts 4:4).

'And the word of God increased; and the number of the disciples multiplied in Jerusalem greatly; and a great company of the priests were obedient to the faith' (Acts 6:7).

'And when they heard it, they glorified the Lord, and said unto him, Thou seest, brother, how many thousands of Jews there are which believe; and they are all zealous of the law' (Acts 21:20).

CHAPTER - 3

WHAT IS REPENTANCE?

Those days, our pastors challenged us with the word of God to prove or bring forth the fruits of repentance.

- Repentance is not an abstract idea or notion that one gives a mental assent to.

- It is not a religious dogma that one believes without any practical consequence on his life and behavior.

- Repentance produces fruits and works in all those who have truly repented. Many people talk about repentance and the effect on the lives of the penitent.

- All who have repented must show the evidence of that repentance by bringing forth the fruits of repentance.

'Bring forth therefore fruits meet for repentance: And think not to say within yourselves, We have Abraham to our father: for I say unto you, that God is able of these stones to raise up children unto Abraham. And now also the axe is laid unto the root of the trees: therefore every tree which bringeth not forth

good fruit is hewn down, and cast into the fire' (Matthew 3:8-10).

- Many great evangelists, pastors, prophets and other titled ministers gather multitudes but cannot show tangible fruits of repentance of the flock.

- There are ministers, pastors who are ministering to many, pastoring many but they refused to be ministered to or pastored.

- They just learn one kingdom language, got occult power and start deceiving people. They boast of their gifts, talents, prosperity, claim to attend bible school, deliverance school, prayer school but they cannot bring forth any fruit of their acclaimed repentance.

- They exact people, tell lies with God's name, prophesy falsely to take members money. Most of them are jobless, lazy and possessed by evil spirits. Prodigal sons and daughters that refuse to repent.

- True repentance leads to a change of conduct, change of mind and must produce a change of action.

- It is not a mere change of opinion; it goes much deeper to bring real reformation of life. Repentance consists of a radical change of mind about God, sin, about self and about the world.

- Previously, sin was delighted in, but now it is hated and mourned over.

- Previously, self was esteemed, but now it is abhorred.

- Previously, you are of the world and his friendship was sought and prized, now your hearts have been diverted from the world and you regard it as your enemy.

- Repentance softens the hard soil of the soul and makes it receptive to the gospel seed.

- To repent is to confess and forsake all known sins.

  'He that covereth his sins shall not prosper: but whoso confesseth and forsaketh them shall have mercy' (Proverbs 28:13).

- Repentance is turning away from sin, turning of heart against sin, change of heart concerning sin.

- Without true repentance, you cannot believe in Christ to be saved.

- Mental acknowledgement of Christ is not faith in Christ. The heart that clings to sin cannot truly exercise faith in Christ.

  'And I will lay it waste: it shall not be pruned, nor digged; but there shall come up briers and thorns: I will also command the clouds that they rain no rain upon it. For the vineyard of the LORD of hosts is the house of Israel, and the men of Judah his pleasant plant: and he looked for judgment, but behold oppression; for righteousness, but behold a cry' (Isaiah 5:6-7).

- To have faith in Christ is to put your complete trust in Him for forgiveness, peace and reconciliation with God.

- When you repent and believe in Christ, you are saved. To be secured in Christ, you must continue following Christ, obeying His words.

- There is no security for the rebellious or sinning Christian.

- The foundation of security is the grace of God and the evidence of grace is continual victory over sin, the flesh and the world.

- True repentance produces always the fruits of righteousness and new life.

  '*I have heard of thee by the hearing of the ear: but now mine eye seeth thee. Wherefore I abhor myself, and repent in dust and ashes*' (Job 42:5).

- If you repent truly, you discontinue from your old ways of evil word, like jokes, old use of sinful slangs and conversation, evil business tricks.

- If you remain cold and lukewarm in spiritual matters, identify yourself with the impenitent unrepentant world, you are not born again.

If you are born-again, you will abhor detestable sins like the following -

1. Pride – (Proverbs 6:16-17, 16:18-19, 21:4, Mark 7:20-23, 1Timothy 3:6, James 4:6).

2. Lying – (Proverbs 6:17, 11:1, 19:9, Ephesians 4:25, Revelation 21:8).

3. Murder – (Proverbs 6:17, Romans 1:28-32, Matthew 5:21-22, 1John 3:15).

4. Evil imaginations and plans – (Proverbs 6:18, Micah 2:1-3, Job 5:12).

5. Mischief and wickedness – (Proverbs 6:12-15, 18, Isaiah 59:1-8, Acts 13:10-11).

6. Perjury – (Proverbs 6:19, 19:5, 25:18, Exodus 23:1, Deuteronomy 19:16-21).

7. Sowing discord – (Proverbs 6:12-15, 19, 16:28, 2 Thessalonians 3:11, 1Timothy 5:13).

8. Adultery and fornication – (Proverbs 6:25-35, 7:24-27, Job 31:9-12, Mark 7:20-23, Acts 15:29, 1Corinthians 6:9-10, Revelation 2:20-23).

9. Stealing – (Ephesians 4:29, Psalms 12:3, 52:2-4, Proverbs 16:27-28, 26:22, Matthew 12:34-37).

10. Bitterness and wrath – (Ephesians 4:31, Hebrews 12:15-17, James 3:14-16).

11. Anger and clamor – (Ephesians 4:31, Psalm 37:8, Proverbs 6:32, Mathew 5:22).

12. Malice – (Ephesians 4:3, Colossians 3:8, 1Peter 2:1).

13. Grieving the Holy Spirit – (Ephesians 4:30, Isaiah 63:10, Acts 5:3, 7:51).

14. Uncleanness – (Ephesians 5:3, Romans 1:23-24, 6:21, 1Thessalonians 4:7).

15. Covetousness – (Ephesians 5:3, Colossians 3:5, Exodus 20:17, Ezekiel 33:31, Luke 12:15).

16. Filthiness – (Ephesians 5:4, James 1:21, 2Peter 2:10, Psalms 53:1-4).

17. Foolish talking – (Ephesians 5:4, James 1:26-27, Proverbs 10:19, 1Peter 3:10).

18. Jesting – (Ephesians 5:4, Proverbs 26:18-19).

BEGINNING OF CHURCH'S LUKEWARMNESS

Like I said earlier, the last group of people in my village, the idol worshippers and the churchgoers, who were not born again later joined, I mean idol worshippers and unrepentant churchgoers. The churchgoers dominated them, compelled them to join them to church. Join the zone, get baptized, and start taking Holy Communion.

The youth among them literally forced their old parents, real idol worshippers to follow them to church, forced them to wed at old age and join the zone.

Once you meet up, get baptized in water, you become a member and if you die, the zonal branch will bury you, pray high-level prayers for you and assure their living members that the dead went to heaven. The priest will pray on the grave, anoint it and the deceived members will believe that he went to heaven. Heaven became very cheap and as they go to church, belonged to a particular zone, they still worshipped their idols freely. Most of their priests are in modern cult but they practice biblical idolatry. Surprisingly, the youth and women among them began to read the bible, form groups, clap hands in their groups and speak in tongues like Pentecostals. Few of them, among, the youth were ordained as priests and began to preach like Pentecostals, speak in tongues.

With time, everyone began to go to church. The church elders, senior ordained priests and bishops tried to stop them but could not. Now, everyone carry bible, preach, pray, clap hands, speak in tongues and perform miracles. There is confusion everywhere because everyone, each party, both the Pentecostals, believed that they are children of God. Everyone speak the same Christian language, praise God, God bless you, sing the same song and heal the sick.

> 'And Moses and Aaron went in unto Pharaoh, and they did so as the LORD had commanded: and Aaron cast down his rod before Pharaoh, and before his servants, and it became a serpent. Then Pharaoh also called the wise men and the sorcerers: now the magicians of Egypt, they also did in like manner with their enchantments. For they cast down every man his rod, and they became serpents: but Aaron's rod swallowed up their rods. And he hardened Pharaoh's heart, that he hearkened not unto them; as the LORD had said' (Exodus 7:10-13).

Moses and Aaron were in one side, with a rod while Pharaoh, his wise men, the sorcerers and magicians were in one side with their enchantment. Both produced result and made Pharaoh to harden his heart. Both parties separated and continued with what they believed, challenging themselves from time to time.

'And Moses and Aaron did so, as the LORD commanded; and he lifted up the rod, and smote the waters that were in the river, in the sight of Pharaoh, and in the sight of his servants; and all the waters that were in the river were turned to blood. And the fish that was in the river died; and the river stank, and the Egyptians could not drink of the water of the river; and there was blood throughout all the land of Egypt. And the magicians of Egypt did so with their enchantments: and Pharaoh's heart was hardened, neither did he hearken unto them; as the LORD had said' (Exodus 7:20-22).

'And the LORD spake unto Moses, Say unto Aaron, Stretch forth thine hand with thy rod over the streams, over the rivers, and over the ponds, and cause frogs to come up upon the land of Egypt. And Aaron stretched out his hand over the waters of Egypt; and the frogs came up, and covered the land of Egypt. And the magicians did so with their enchantments, and brought up frogs upon the land of Egypt' (Exodus 8:5-7).

'And the LORD said unto Moses, Rise up early in the morning, and stand before Pharaoh; lo, he cometh forth to the water: and say unto him, Thus saith the LORD, Let my people go, that they may serve me. Else, if thou wilt not let my people go, behold, I will send swarms of flies upon thee, and upon thy servants, and upon thy people, and into thy houses: and the houses of the Egyptians shall be full of swarms of flies, and also the ground whereon they are. And I will sever in that day the land of Goshen, in which my people dwell, that no swarms of flies shall be there; to the end thou mayest know that I am the LORD in the midst of the earth. And I will put a division between my people and thy people: tomorrow shall this sign be' (Exodus 8:20-23).

'And it came to pass on the morrow, that the evil spirit from God came upon Saul, and he *prophesied in the midst of the house: and David played with his hand, as at other times: and there was a javelin in Saul's hand. And Saul cast the javelin; for he said, I will smite David even to the wall with it. And David avoided out of his presence twice'* (1Samuel 18:10-11).

As I searched the scriptures, I discovered that every genuine thing that God does, Satan would try to bring along counterfeit to confuse the minds of men, deceive his followers and harden their hearts. Moses and Aaron's group, the Pentecostals, continued until God gave them victory, their opponent, confessed that power pass power.

'And these are the names of the sons of Levi according to their generations; Gershon, and Kohath, and Merari: and the years of the life of Levi were an hundred thirty and seven years. The sons of Gershon; Libni, and Shimi, according to their families. And the sons of Kohath; Amram, and Izhar, and Hebron, and Uzziel: and the years of the life of Kohath were an hundred thirty and three years. And the sons of Merari;

Mahali and Mushi: these are the families of Levi according to their generations' (Exodus 8:16-19).

But instead of the Pentecostals of our time to continue, they compromised and left the source of their power, which is preaching, teaching and discipleship. They followed the servants of Pharaoh, the sorcerers, the magicians and continued in competition. They compromised, modified their preaching, their teaching, bowed to the pressure groups, influenced by Satan and self who judge things carnally by outward appearance only. They craved for popularity, praise of men and they backslide.

'*Woe unto you, when all men shall speak well of you! For so did their fathers to the false prophets'* (Luke 6:26).

Today, everyone is seeking for prophecy, no one is ready to preach, teach and tell people the truth. Once you can prophecy, tell people what they want to hear, even if you are a devil, they follow you anywhere you go. Before, ministers were likened to -

Ambassadors (Ephesians 3:20),

Servants (Philippians 1, Galatians 1:10),

Builders (1Corinthians 3:10),

Chosen Vessel (Acts 9:15, 2 Corinthians 4:7),

Stewards (1 Corinthians 4:1-2, Luke 16:1-2)

Ministers of the New Testament (1Corinthians 3:6, 4:1-2).

But today, reverse is the case, our modern ministers are small gods, occult grandmasters and if you question their actions, they will curse you. They forget that Christ in the body carried out a divinely appointed mission. He mixed up, humbled himself and revealed the love and grace of God to man. He gave up everything – position, right, glory, life to reconcile man to God. With that mission accomplished, He left the world and went to the father in heaven.

When He left, He left the church behind to carry out and continue the same mission to reveal God to man through Christ and reconcile man to God through Christ to the whole of humanity. Every member of the church is expected to do the will of God in carrying on the mission of Christ. Jesus went to individuals, preached in the cities, sent his disciples. They evangelized, edify, witness, worship, testified, taught and disciple. They practiced personal evangelism and their preaching produced conviction of sin but today, reverse is the case. The whole church has backslide, seeking for personal gain.

> *'The fruit of the righteous is a tree of life; and he that winneth souls is wise'* (<u>Proverbs 11:30</u>).

Churches are no longer winning soul; they are winning people's money. The word win is a military term. To win a city is to lay siege on it and take it. It calls for skill, patience, bravery and endurance. It is also an occupational term. Like a fisherman, the soul winner, in the face of all kinds of weather and risks, applies himself to the task of skillfully bringing the sinner to Christ. Moreover, it is a matrimonial term. To win a soul to Christ is like winning a bride for the bridegroom and it takes prayer, affection, attention, sincerity, sacrifice and honest communication.

THIS IS THE CONSEQUENCE OF BACKSLIDING ELDERS, PENTECOSTALISM:

- They became covetous (Genesis 13:10),

- They compromised (Genesis 13:12-13),

- They were influenced by the worldly society (Hosea 7:8-9, 1 Samuel 8:19-20, 2 Kings 17:15),

- Pride entered them (Proverbs 16:18),

- They lusted for the flesh (Nehemiah 13:26, Judges 16:14-20),

- They entered into self-indulgence (Genesis 9:1, 20-21);

- They loved money (1Timothy 6:9-10, John 13:29, Joshua 7:20-21),

- They loved the world (2 Timothy 4:10),

- They cared so much for this world (Mark 4:18-19),

- They used authority inordinately (2 Chronicles 16:9-12, 26:15-20),

- They entered into unbelief (Hebrews 3:12, 78:18-22, 2 Kings 1:2-4),

- They became prayer less (Matthew 26:40-41, 58).

- They created vacancy in the office of leadership in the church (Exodus 32:1, Judges 17:6),

- They brought bad examples in the church (Isaiah 56:10-12),

- They became immoral (1Samuel 7:12-17, 22, 8:10-21, Jeremiah 23:9-16),

- They allowed false prophecies to come into the church (Jeremiah 2:8, 10:21, 12:10, Isaiah 28:7),

- They preferred compromising preachers (Numbers 14:1-4, 2 Timothy 4:3-4, Isaiah 30:9-10),

- They desired temporary blessings above spiritual blessings (John 6:10-15, 25-35, 60, 66, Psalms 106:13-16),

- They encouraged partial obedience, unfaithfulness and insecurity (1Samuel 15:7-11, 16:14, Acts 5:1-10, Revelation 22:18-19),

- They preferred prosperity and abundance without holiness and zeal (Deuteronomy 32:5, 6, 15, Jeremiah 22:21-22, Revelation 3:14-20),

- They allowed strange preachers with false doctrines (Jeremiah 5:31, Hosea 4:6).

- The worse, they fight over positions, ordained themselves with the highest ordination in the church without God's approval.

- They also ordained unconverted women, children without experience to lead the church

   'As for my people, children are their oppressors, and women rule over them. O my people, they which lead thee cause thee to err, and destroy the way of thy paths... What mean ye that ye beat my people to pieces, and grind the faces of the poor? saith the Lord GOD of hosts' (Isaiah 3:12, 15).

   'But there was none like unto Ahab, which did sell himself to work wickedness in the sight of the LORD, whom Jezebel his wife stirred up' (1Kings 21:25).

Immediately these prophetess, young boys with talents got into leadership without much knowledge about God, his word and ways, they conspired against the church, break away, began to prophesy. Multitudes from the church followed them, especially youths and the women.

'Thus saith the LORD, Stand ye in the ways, and see, and ask for the old paths, where is the good way, and walk therein, and ye shall find rest for your souls. But they said, We will not walk therein. Also I set watchmen over you, saying, Hearken to the sound of the trumpet. But they said, We will not hearken' (Jeremiah 6:16-17).

The Pentecostal youths followed suit and became worse, break the congregation and took away the members.

These youths, full of strength left without permission, instruction, commission and blessings from the leaders. The leaders cursed them, prayed against them and destroyed their ministries because they took away the people that pay them tithes. The church became poor, left with few members and leaders with big tithes. God withdrew His presence from the church and they experienced unanswered prayers. They started suffering under the power of darkness causing sickness, mysterious deaths and all manner of problems.

God in His infinite mercy call those youths to stand on the truth of God's word, ask for the old paths, the good way, walk therein, find rest for their souls and break out from the curses of the elders they left but they refused. Because of their in experience, zeal without knowledge and curse from their abandoned leaders, they refused to obey God.

> 'But this thing commanded I them, saying, Obey my voice, and I will be your God, and ye shall be my people: and walk ye in all the ways that I have commanded you, that it may be well unto you. But they hearkened not, nor inclined their ear, but walked in the counsels and in the imagination of their evil heart, and went backward, and not forward... Yet they hearkened not unto me, nor inclined their ear, but hardened their neck: they did worse than their fathers. Therefore thou shalt speak all these words unto them; but they will not hearken to thee: thou shalt also call unto them; but they will not answer thee' (Jeremiah 7:23-24, 26-27).

God left them and they became an outcast, captive, leper, their names was removed from the book of life and God forsook them (Exodus 32:33), the wrath of God came upon them (Ezra 8:22, Job 34:26-27), God rejected them (1 Samuel 15:22-26, 1Corinthians 9:27). They became spiritually dead (1Timothy 5:14-16, Ezekiel 18:24, 26), they became exposed to demonic attacks (1Samuel 16:14, John 13:26-27, Luke 11:24-26). They became enslaved to Satan (1Timothy 5:15), their consciences were seared with a rod of iron (1Timothy 4:1, 22). Like Saul, they went and sought for help from a witch doctor and occults (1Samuel 28:6-7).

In the process of looking for solution for their problems, these youths enter into covenant with evil spirits. Some died physically while the remaining that came out alive died spiritually. They are the ones that you see around the cities pulling cloud.

Gathering the properties in the cities, building mansions, cathedrals without building lives. They drive the best cars, knows the people that matters, deceiving and being deceived. They claim to have power to see, hear, heal, prosper and deliver people but they are liars, their power is powerless and their deliverance is not delivered. They are swindlers, carnal, full of greed, pride, anger, jealousy, covetous, unfaithful and possessed with the spirit of mammon, always talking about seed sowing, money.

They are irresponsible, unfaithful in marriage without any discipline. They do not cast out demons; they transfer them, suspend their actions for a while or see problems without giving you solutions. They draw cloud; render the archbishops, bishops and old prophets in Laodicea useless without members. Their churches and remaining members are lukewarm. Laodicea church was abandoned and is the only church out of the seven churches in Asia that had no point of praise or commendation.

Religion became a substitute for reality and Luke warmness characterized the whole church, not even a trace of faithful few as in Sardis was found among them. They were all lukewarm, neither cold nor hot. They were all wretched, miserable, poor, blind and naked spiritually. They were all congregation of sinners, backsliders professing to be Christian leaders but they were vile, sinful, and pitiable, without the robe of righteousness. Most of their leaders were in cults, witchcraft groups and very insincere, religious, hypocritical and harder to win to Christ than cold, irreligious sinners.

> '*I know thy works, that thou art neither cold nor hot: I would thou wert cold or hot. So then because thou art lukewarm, and neither cold nor hot, I will spue thee out of my mouth. Because thou sayest, I am rich, and increased with goods, and have need of nothing; and knowest not that thou art wretched, and miserable, and poor, and blind, and naked*' (Revelation 3:15-17).

Even with their condition, backslidden state, Christ wrote to them. The letter was addressed to all, the elders and the youth ministers. Christ was and still, is pictured as standing at the door of every heart, church knocking and asking for entrance.

> '*I counsel thee to buy of me gold tried in the fire, that thou mayest be rich; and white raiment, that thou mayest be clothed, and that the*

shame of thy nakedness do not appear; and anoint thine eyes with eyesalve, that thou mayest see. As many as I love, I rebuke and chasten: be zealous therefore, and repent. Behold, I stand at the door, and knock: if any man hear my voice, and open the door, I will come in to him, and will sup with him, and he with me' (Revelation 3:18-20).

Luke warmness brings shame, reproach and disgrace. It brings spiritual pollutions, decay, and all manner of poverty, uncleanness, nakedness, spiritual blindness and chastisement. Christ's counsel to the lukewarm church in Laodicea is to repent. He promises to come back to deliver them, anyone of them who will hear, open the door of his heart, church, sup with Him and be with Him.

The letter is to the whole church and individual who will respond to His request, no matter how bad you are, how wicked you are and how far you have gone away from God, you can still be delivered. If you can leave your evil way of life, dubious way of life and submit to God's deliverance program, you will be delivered, set free and restored back to God. To please God means to repent, confess and forsake all your sins and you will be forgiven.

> 'Cast away from you all your transgressions, whereby ye have transgressed; and make you a new heart and a new spirit: for why will ye die, O house of Israel?' (Ezekiel 18:31).

> 'Say unto them, As I live, saith the Lord GOD, I have no pleasure in the death of the wicked; but that the wicked turn from his way and live: turn ye, turn ye from your evil ways; for why will ye die, O house of Israel?' (Ezekiel 33:11).

You can disown your transgressions in a moment of time; receive a new heart, a new spirit and a brand new life now if you repent. God is not happy the way things are going in your life, your suffering and hardship. He is not willing or has any pleasure in your death. What God wants from you is to turn from your wicked ways, evil pursuits to avoid death. What God demands from you are not difficult, impossible or what you cannot do. He is willing and determined to help you if you want.

'And saying, Repent ye: for the kingdom of heaven is at hand' (Matthew 3:2).

'And the times of this ignorance God winked at; but now commandeth all men everywhere to repent' (Acts 17:30).

You can enter into the kingdom of heaven while you are here on earth. Part of heaven's provision can be made available to you while you are still here on earth. It can start now, if you repent with all your heart and decide to serve God only.

'Now then we are ambassadors for Christ, as though God did beseech you by us: we pray you in Christ's stead, be ye reconciled to God' (2 Corinthians 5:20).

God has decided to forget all your evil acts against Him and humankind. It is a time of your ignorance if you can repent now and forsake all your sins. He wants to empower you with true power, everlasting power, unstoppable anointing and abundant life. Not all hope is lost for a repentant sinner. Though your past conducts and profession had been so disgusting and offensive, yet if you repent, seek things above, not on things on earth and open the door of your heart to receive the waiting knocking Christ, salvation and heaven will be yours.

> 'And he that overcometh, and keepeth my works unto the end, to him will I give power over the nations' (Revelation 2:26).

> 'To him that overcometh will I grant to sit with me in my throne, even as I also overcame, and am set down with my Father in his throne. He that hath an ear, let him hear what the Spirit saith unto the churches' (Revelation 3:21-22).

You need to understand that there is a battle going on against you and Christ is standing by to help you to overcome. There is a lasting crown for you if you overcome. You will start enjoying divine presence, divine defense and divine provisions. To hear other words, read other letters and fail in this very one is the worst failure. You need to be fast; open your ears hear and do what the Holy Spirit expects of you. If you need deliverance in any area of your life, that is the purpose of this letter. Christ is here, with all determination, in all

His power to deliver any congregation that is ready for deliverance.

> '*And I saw, and behold a white horse: and he that sat on him had a bow; and a crown was given unto him: and he went forth conquering, and to conquer*' (Revelation 6:2).

> '*And every man that striveth for the mastery is temperate in all things. Now they do it to obtain a corruptible crown; but we an incorruptible*' (1 Corinthians 9:25).

> '*Henceforth there is laid up for me a crown of righteousness, which the Lord, the righteous judge, shall give me at that day: and not to me only, but unto all them also that love his appearing*' (2 Timothy 4:8).

The power that the devil, the occult, his agents have given you may be to gather few cloud, two million people out of millions of tens in your city. He may not give you the power to gather up to 1% of the people in the city where you live in. You just gather few thousands and you are happy. You may be your church's deliverance minister, pastor or bishop of three million members.

Christ's letter says, if you overcome and keep His works unto the end, He will give you power, not to have rule over just America, one nation, but power over nations. Everything in that nation, the banks, the oil companies are yours. What are you benefitting in the occult, witchcraft group that you cannot get in nations? It is ignorance, foolishness to remain in bondage when your deliverer is just by your door knocking.

What are you looking for that Christ cannot give you or cannot do for you? This is your opportunity to get full help and full deliverance. Jesus, the man in white horse, with absolute holiness and power to set you free from your captors is standing by your door. His crown is everlasting and other powers that has crown, gives crowns, bows at His feet. Why would you seek for any crown from evil source when Christ is saying to you, come and take my crown, an everlasting crown that cannot fade away?

'Blessed is the man that endureth temptation: for when he is tried, he shall receive the crown

of life, which the Lord hath promised to them that love him' (James 1:12).

'And when the chief Shepherd shall appear, ye shall receive a crown of glory that fadeth not away' (1 Peter 5:4).

Whatever you can do to reject what you receive from the devil, from the occult or satanic agents, do so now. The reason is that the letter you are reading now is from Christ. A line in that letter is promising you an incorruptible crown that can never fade away. This is a crown of righteousness from the righteous judge, the great Amen with everlasting seal.

'Behold, I come quickly: hold that fast which thou hast, that no man take thy crown' (Revelation 3:11).

'The four and twenty elders fall down before him that sat on the throne, and worship him that liveth for ever and ever, and cast their crowns before the throne, saying' (Revelation 4:10)

'And he said unto him, Well, thou good servant: because thou hast been faithful in a very little, have thou authority over ten cities' (Luke 19:17).

The devil can give you crown or crowns, promise you heaven and earth but remember, he is a liar and there is no truth in him. Christ is the truth, the way and life, His promises are yes and Amen. He has promised you in this program crown of life, you can join the overcomers today. If you love Christ, you will be happy to please Him, make Him happy and be proud of you. To love Him, you must keep His word, obey His word and be ready to pay any price to keep His commandment.

All the glory attached to whatever the devil has given you, the position and power you now enjoy is temporary. In the kingdom of darkness, whatever they promise you is not up to the glory that is attached to crown of glory that Christ will give you and has promised you. You cannot receive Christ's glory if you still keep Satan's glory. It is not possible to serve God and the devil at the same time.

Crowns are exchangeable, it is better to exchange the devil's crown, gifts, blessings, power with what God gives than to do otherwise. It is better to receive everlasting crown from the everlasting Christ than to receive a temporary crown that will bring tears into your eyes later. It is better to receive crown from the one that sits on the throne than the one that was over thrown from heaven. It is better to receive crown from Him that is worshipped and liveth forever and ever than to receive it from a failure like the devil. It is disgracing, worst to receive any crown from any person, group that is less than the devil, his agents, occult or witch doctor. What an insult to submit to the devil, his agents or any evil group.

The leaders of the church in Laodicea were struggling for position in the city and lost the church to the spirit of Luke warmness. You do not need to struggle for anything, be it power, position or any blessing. The power you have now may be just for one place, a city church branch; Christ's promise to overcomers is authority over cities. If you become an overcomer, a saint, Christ's promise is to empower you to judge the world, not just where you are now. You will have power to talk to any part of the world and they will obey you.

Do not allow the devil or one small occult you belong to keep limiting you. You have a promise to be established globally in whatever you are doing. Your business, job, profession will take you to the world, all places and advertise you beyond your location. What you have now is too small; the smallest thing to compare with what Christ wants to do in your life, if you join the overcomers. Why do you choose to deal with small matters, blessings, contract, open door, anointing and smallest problems when you have the opportunity to go worldwide, limitless and without boundary?

I counsel you; join the overcomers, the winners on the Lord's side. If you know what God have for you, you will ignore any suffering before you now, face any opposition against your becoming an overcomer and with your last strength, fight to the end. The glory before you, waiting for you to overcome is beyond explanation, more than what any occult group can offer and the whole world put together. Are you afraid of the devil; are you under his threats, or his agents and all the evil forces put together?

Listen, whatever they can do is likened to light affliction, small problem, trouble, a moment to compare to the external, everlasting, continuous and voluminous weight of glory that Christ is standing before you to give. Ignore everything, all things and press forward to be an overcomer and you will not suffer the rest of your life, here and in eternity. The overcomers will share in Christ's honor and triumph. Do you know what that offers means? It is beyond me to explain because it is better experienced than to say. The church of our time, ministers and members need deliverance that will lead to everlasting inheritance.

Thank You So Much

Beloved, I hope you enjoyed this book as much as I believe God has touched your heart today. I cannot thank you enough for your continued support for this prayer ministry.

I appreciate you so much for spending time to read this wonderful prayer book, and if you have an extra second, I would love to hear what you think about this book.

Please, do share your testimonies with me by sending an email to me at prayermadu@yahoo.com, also in Facebook at www.facebook.com/prayermadueke. I invite you to my website at www.prayermadueke.com to view many other books I have written on various issues of life, especially on marriage, family, sexual problems and money.

I will be delighted to partner with you also in organized crusades, ceremonies, marriages and marriage seminars, special events, church ministration and fellowship for the advancement of God's kingdom here on earth.

Thank you again, and I wish you nothing less than success in life.

God bless you.

Prayer M. Madueke

Books by Prayer M. Madueke

- 21/40 Nights Of Decrees And Your Enemies Will Surrender
- Tears In Prison
- 35 Special Dangerous Decrees
- More Kingdoms To Conquer
- Prayer Riots To Overthrow Divorce
- Prayers To Get Married Happily
- Prayers To Keep Your Marriage Out Of Troubles
- Prayers For Conception And Power To Retain
- Prayer Retreat – Prayers To Possess Your Year
- Prayers For Nation Building
- Organized Student In A Disorganized School
- Welcome To Campus
- Alone With God (10 Series)
- 40 Prayer Giants
- Prayers For Marriage And Family
- Prayers For Academic Success
- Alone With God- Prayers For Finance

- Special Prayers In His Presence
- Prayers For Good Health
- Prayer Retreat
- Prayers For Children And Youths
- Youths, May I Have Your Attention Please?
- Alone With God- Prayers For Successful Career
- General Prayers For Nation Building
- Prayers Against Satanic Oppression
- Prayers For A Successful Career
- Prayers For Deliverance
- Prayers For Financial Breakthrough
- Prayers For Overcoming Attitude Problems
- Contemporary Politician's Prayers For Nation Building
- Veteran Politician's Prayer For Nation Building
- Prayers To Marry Without Delay
- Prayers For Marriages In Distress
- Prayers To Prevent Separation Of Couples
- Prayers For Restoration Of Peace In Marriage
- Prayers To Triumph Over Divorce
- Prayers To Heal Broken Relationship

- Prayers To Pray During Courtship
- Prayers For Your Wedding
- Prayers To Pray During Honeymoon
- Prayers For Newly Married Couples
- Prayers To Experience Love In Your Marriage
- Prayers For Fertility In Your Marriage
- Prayers To Conceive And Bear Children
- Prayers To Preserve Your Marriage
- Prayers For Pregnant Women
- Prayers To Retain Your Pregnancy
- Prayers To Overcome Miscarriage
- Prayers To End A Prolonged Pregnancy
- Prayers To Deliver Your Child Safely
- Prayers To Raise Godly Children
- Prayers To Overcome An Evil Habit
- Prayers For Your Children's Deliverance
- Prayers To Live An Excellent Life
- Prayers For College And University Students
- Prayers For Success And Examinations
- Prayers For An Excellent Job
- Prayers For A Job Interview

- Prayers To Progress In Your Career
- Prayers For Healthy Living And Long Life
- Prayers To Live And End Your Life Well
- Prayers For Breakthrough In Your Business
- Prayers For All Manner Of Sickness And Disease
- Prayers For A Happy Married Life
- Prayers To Buy A Home And Settle Down
- Prayers To Receive Financial Miracles
- Prayers For Christmas
- Prayers For Widows And Orphans
- Prayers Against Premature Death
- Prayers For Sound Sleep And Rest
- Prayer Campaign For Nigeria
- Fall And Rise Of The Igbo Nation
- Because You Are Living Abroad
- Americans, May I Have Your Attention Please
- Pray For Your Country

Made in the USA
Monee, IL
15 October 2021